Bilingual Edition

READING POWER

Edición Bilingüe

(**Extreme Machines**)

Long Limousines

Limosinas largas

Scott P. Werther

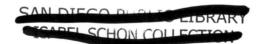

The Rosen Publishing Group's
PowerKids Press™ & **Buenas Letras**™
New York

Published in 2003 by The Rosen Publishing Group, Inc.
29 East 21st Street, New York, NY 10010
Copyright © 2003 by The Rosen Publishing Group, Inc.

First Bilingual Edition 2003
First Edition in English 2002

Book Design: Erica Clendening
Photo Credits: Front cover © Angelo Cavalli/ImageBank; pp. 4–5 (top half of page), 20–21 (top half of page) © Artville, LLC.; pp. 4–5, 6–7, 10 (inset), 10–11, 12–13, 14–15, 15 (inset) © Craftsman Limousine, Inc.; pp. 8–9 © Jay Ohrberg Star Cars; pp. 16–17 © Hummer Style; pp. 18–19 © Reuters NewMedia Inc./Corbis; pp. 20–21 © Jay Thomas/International Stock; Back cover © Scott Barrow/International Stock

Werther , Scott P
Long Limousines/limosinas largas/Scott P. Werther ; traducción al español: Spanish Educational Publishing
p. cm. — (Extreme Machines)
Includes bibliographical references and index.
ISBN 0-8239-6889-8 (lib. bdg.)
1. Limousines—Juvenile literature. [1. Limousines 2. Spanish Language Materials—Bilingual.] I. Title.
TG106.K63 T48 2001
624'.5—dc21

2001000599

Manufactured in the United States of America

Contents _____

_____ # Contenido

This is a limousine. It is a very long car that can hold many people.

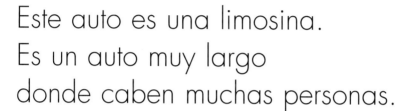

Este auto es una limosina.
Es un auto muy largo
donde caben muchas personas.

Many limousines have seats for more than ten people. Regular cars seat only five people.

La limosina tiene asientos
para más de diez personas.
En un auto común sólo caben
cinco personas.

The longest limousine in the world is 100 feet (30m) long. It can hold 72 people!

La limosina más larga del mundo
mide 100 pies (30m) de largo.
¡En esta limosina caben
72 personas!

Limousines are made by cutting a regular car or truck in half. Then, a long middle section is added to the car or truck.

Para hacer una limosina,
se corta un auto o camioneta
común en dos. Después se le
agrega la parte larga en el medio.

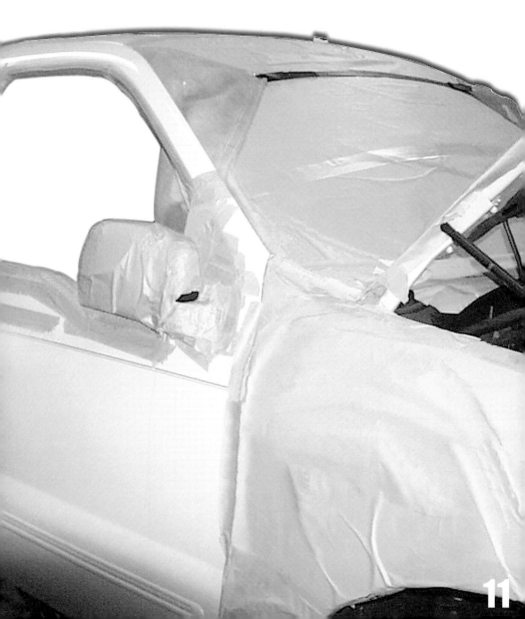

Sides are added to the middle section of the limousine. Windows and doors are put into the sides.

Se le ponen los lados
a la parte del medio.
Se ponen ventanas y puertas
en los lados.

Seats are added after the limousine is put together. Many limousines even have fancy mirrors and televisions.

Cuando la limosina está armada, se le ponen los asientos.
Muchas limosinas tienen espejos en el techo y televisores.

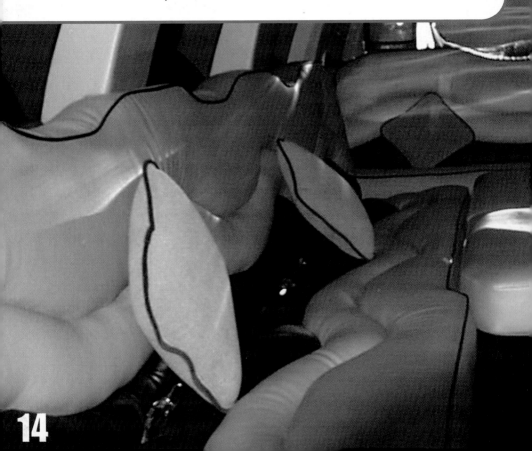

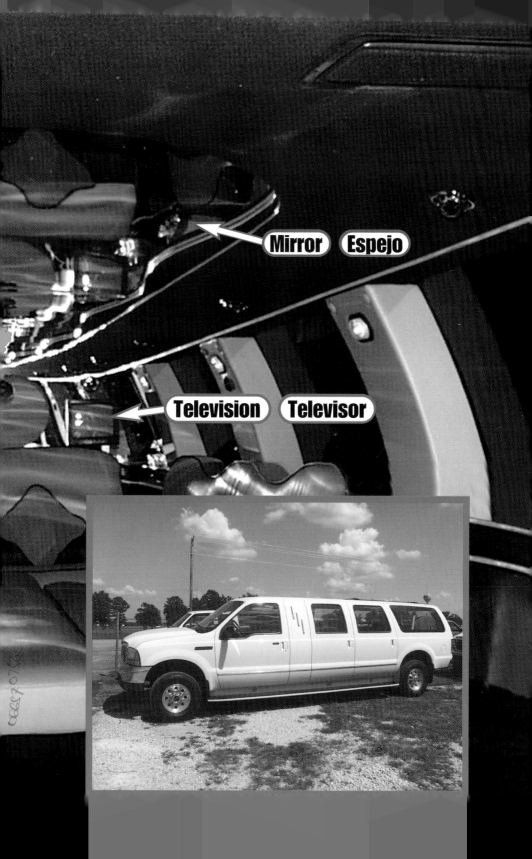

Mirror **Espejo**

Television **Televisor**

Some limousines have tinted windows so that no one can see who is inside.

Algunas limosinas tienen
ventanas oscuras para que
no se pueda ver hacia dentro.

The president of the United States has a special limousine. It has a very thick roof and thick doors to keep him safe.

El presidente de los Estados Unidos
tiene una limosina especial.
El techo y las puertas son muy
gruesos para que no corra peligro.

People use limousines for many different reasons. One reason is that it is exciting to travel in a limousine!

Las limosinas se usan para
distintas cosas.
¡Es emocionante viajar en limosina!

Glossary

fancy (fan-see) not plain or simple

limousine (lihm-uh-zeen) a car or truck that has been changed to hold a lot of people

tinted (tihnt-uhd) colored or darkened

Glosario

limosina (la) auto o camioneta larga donde entran muchas personas

pie (el) medida de longitud

Resources / Recursos

Here are more books to read about long limousines:
Otros libros que puedes leer sobre limosinas largas:

The World's Most Exotic Cars
by John Martin
Capstone Press (1995)

Encyclopedia of Cars
Chris Horton, editor
Chelsea House (1997)

Word count in English: 160
Número de palabras en español: 146

Index

Índice